The Hemingway Home Cat Coloring Book

Joanna Werynska & Brian Teasley
Copyright © 2023 Joanna Werynska

All rights reserved.

ISBN: 978-1-7332531-3-0

Key West, Florida
USA

This coloring book is dedicated to the legendary Hemingway Home Black Cat named Howard Hughes

MEOW!

Welcome to the coloring book of the world-famous Hemingway Home and Museum cats. **The book features drawings based on actual photographs** taken at the Museum in Key West, Florida by cat lover and tour guide Joanna Werynska. The cats and situations depicted are real. *No cat was harmed in the creation of this book, but one human's arm sustained a small scratch from a playful kitten who liked the camera too much. Kitten and human are both fine.*

Nobel Prize winning author Ernest Hemingway loved cats. He used to say, "One cat just leads to another", so it's more than appropriate there are cats in his former Key West home. All the cats on the property have the polydactyl gene. This means it is possible for them to have extra toes. Cats normally have five toes on their front paws and four on each back paw. Some cats at the Hemingway Home have **six toes** on each of their paws. A few even have seven toes!

More than 50 felines live on the property. Most of them are named after famous people or characters from Mr. Hemingway's time. They are different sizes and have different personalities. They live their purr-fect lives in the lush tropical gardens surrounding the writer's house. They even have their own staff taking care of them!

Polydactyl is not a breed. Any breed can have extra toes. At the Hemingway Home there are Black Cats, Grey Cats, Orange Cats, Tuxedo Cats (black and white cats), White and Black Cats, Calico Cats, and Tabby Cats that are mostly grey with stripes like a tiger. **Now, it is your turn to color them all!**

Book Creators

Joanna was honored to work as a tour guide, ticket seller and cat catcher (if needed) at the Hemingway Home and Museum. In the meantime, she loved spending time with the cats and taking the photographs on which the drawings in this book are based.

You can email Joanna at: J.WERYNSKA@GMAIL.COM

Joanna's husband Brian also proudly worked at the Hemingway Home as a tour guide, kitten walker, cat catcher, gardener, ticket seller, and helped clean the property after a hurricane. He assisted in creating this coloring book, too.

Previous Page and Opposite Page:

Apparently, the museum rules do not apply to the cats. At least that's what Marlene Dietrich thinks. The always elegant black and white cat naps in the Hemingway's living room on the antique pink couch from Paris

Opposite Page:

Three cats - Betty Grable (left - black and white), Joe DiMaggio (upper right - brown tabby), and Daisy Buchanan (lower right - dark brown) enjoy a peaceful nap in air-conditioning atop Mr. Hemingway's bed

Opposite Page:

Betty Grable spends her days posing for pictures while napping in her favorite spot in the window of the main bathroom in the Hemingway House. She is mostly black with intriguing white paws

Opposite Page:

Fluffy, dark-brown, green-eyed, six-toed Daisy Buchanan likes to pose for pictures in Mr. Hemingway's master bedroom. Or maybe she just likes to be comfortable and nap?

Opposite Page:

Marilyn Monroe is a grey tabby cat. She has white paws with extra toes. She likes to show them off while relaxing on a bench on the front porch of the Hemingway House

Opposite Page:

Big brown tabby Joe DiMaggio keeps watch with his lovely green eyes on the front porch of the house. Perhaps he is trying to figure out which visitors might have cat treats?

Opposite Page:

Daisy Buchanan, a dark brown tabby with fluffy paws, is one of the most stylish cats in the Museum. Here, she shows off her freshly-made lion haircut while posing proudly next to the fountain in front of the house

Opposite Page:

Shoeless Joe Jackson (black and white with a pink nose, underneath the chair) sneaks up on Hercules (big grey tabby mixed with white) to see if Hercules really has seven toes on his big white front paw

Opposite Page:

Etta James (grey tabby with white) looks for an audience to meow jazz to while standing by her favorite staircase. She is a small grey tabby with big green eyes, a white muzzle, and white paws

Opposite Page:

Dark colored big tabby cat Bumby shows off his seven-toed, black-dotted paws while walking on colorful tiles imported by Mr. Hemingway from Havana, Cuba. Bumby has a brown nose, big green eyes, and a black stripe down his back

Opposite Page:

Cream colored Boo Radley tries to pass unnoticed by the cat condominiums on the back of the property. This shy cat has big blue eyes and a pink nose. He is on a path of red Baltimore bricks bought by Mr. Hemingway in the 1930s

Opposite Page:

The beautiful calico named Talulah Bankhead (on the right - mixed grey, white and cream colors) and Captain Stanley Dexter (on the left - handsome orange tabby) have a morning lap of fresh water out of a very original cat water fountain

Opposite Page:

Hemingway is a handsome big tabby with green eyes and a meringue colored belly. The tip of his tail is black. Here he checks from the front porch of the house who is visiting the Museum today. After all, it is his home - so he has to know!

Opposite Page

The kittens are very happy you are going to color them. They want to play with your pencil! In the back row on the left is a shy Boo Radley (beige/cream). In the middle of the back row is Elvis Presley (black). On the right is Bernice Dickson (black and white), in front with his pink paw showing is Lefty Grove (white and orange). Putting his ginger colored tail in the picture is orange tabby Buster Keaton

Opposite Page:

The kittens are always a joy at the Museum. It is a shame they grow so fast. In front is the curious, orange tabby Buster Keaton. His shy creme colored brother Boo Radley hides in the back row on the left. Next to him is black kitten Elvis Presley and the mostly black colored Bernice Dickson. White and orange Lefty Grove is behind Buster Keaton

Opposite Page:

Mata Hari knows Mr. Hemingway's writing studio is the most important room in the Museum. She always keeps an eye on Papa's Royal portable typewriter. Mata Hari is a grey tabby with white paws, a white nose, and green eyes

Opposite Page:

Making sure her white paws are clean, Etta James sits on the green window sill of the main house. Her long tail and her head are both dark grey

Opposite Page:

Black and white Shoeless Joe Jackson shows off his white extra toe. He has a pink nose with a funny black dot on it, and bright green eyes

Opposite Page:

Grey and white colored Mata Hari is just pretending to be asleep. In fact she observes who is coming to see Mr. Hemingway's typewriter from the bathroom window of the author's writing studio

Opposite Page:

The friendly black cat named Papa watches you from behind some red Baltimore bricks. He has green eyes and is trying to figure out who wants to pet him next. Papa loves to be loved, just like Papa Hemingway

Opposite Page:

The small black and white cat named Holly Golightly joyfully shows off her short, black bobtail while walking on a path through the garden. She has a funny black spot on her muzzle, too!

Opposite Page:

Big grey and white Hercules has seven toes, but he doesn't want to brag about them right now. He enjoys a break from hunting lizards while lying on a path on the back of the property. Hercules wants you to color his nose pink, eyes green, and part of his muzzle near his right eye dark grey. He is very handsome and he knows it

Opposite Page:

The black cat named Elvis Presley checks to see what is going on in the garden from the top of the cat condominiums. Perhaps he is looking for an audience so he can meow rock and roll to them

Opposite Page:

Legendary black cat Howard Hughes comes out shyly from his nearby dark hole. He is reclusive and shy, but wants you to color him, too

Opposite Page:

Grey tabby Winston Churchill looks quite comfortable while using red Baltimore bricks as a pillow

Opposite Page:

Colorful cat Brigitte Bardot poses languidly on the colorful tiles Mr. Hemingway brought from Havana, Cuba in the 1930s. Her coat is a mix of black, white, and creme colors

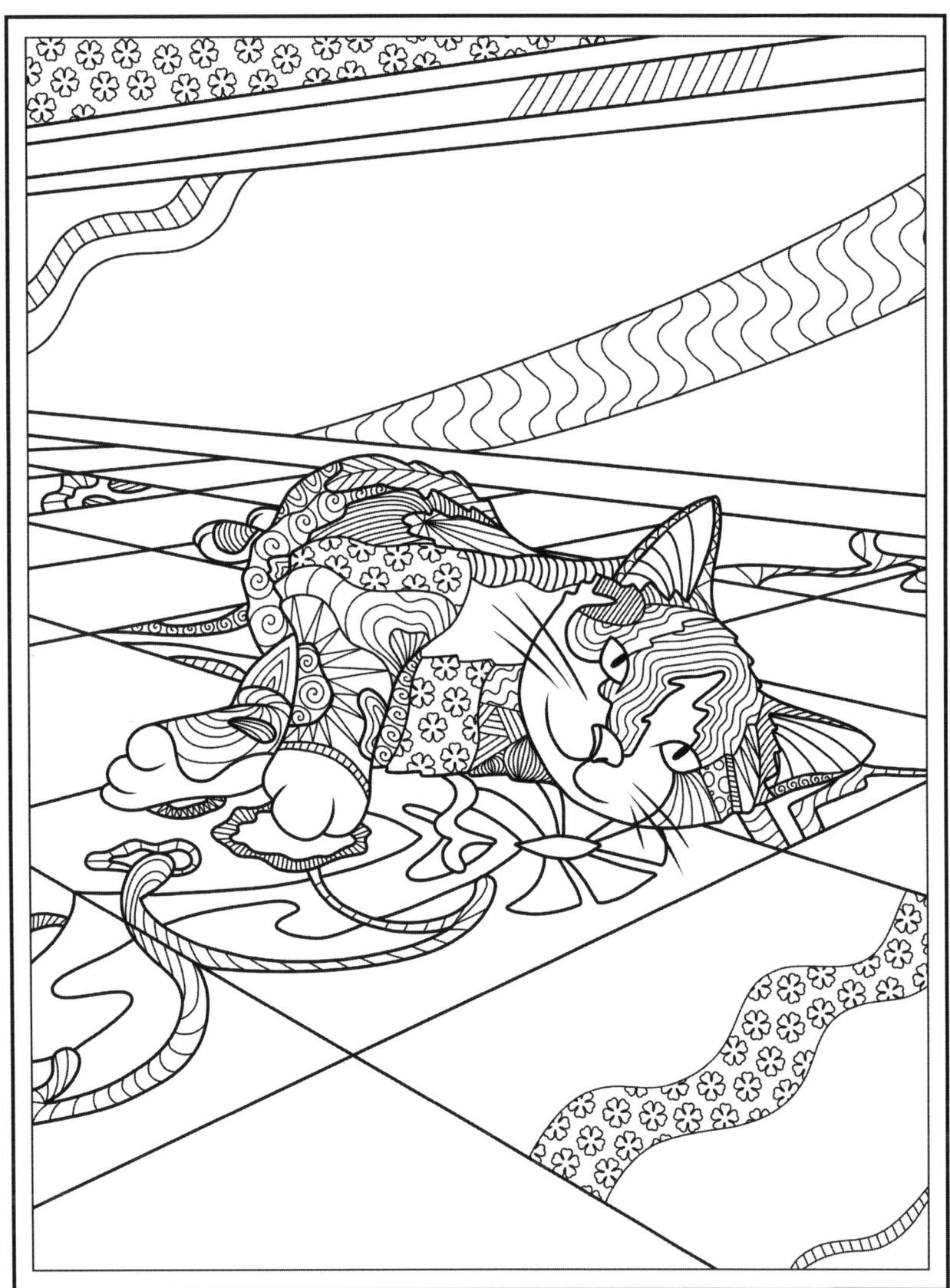

Opposite Page:

The all black colored Howard Hughes comes to say hello to you and shows off his gigantic seven-toed paws while walking past the back of the house

Opposite Page:

Always elegant, tuxedo cat (black and white) Marlene Dietrich crosses her white paws daintily while resting in the garden near the front gate of the property

Opposite Page:

Shirley Temple (left - beige/brown) with her new lion haircut, waits for the bookstore door to open while Lefty Grove (right - white/orange) watches for approaching customers

Opposite Page:

The entrance of the Hemingway Home and Museum in Key West, Florida. A United States National Landmark and Purr-fect home of the World Famous Six-toed Cats!

The Hemingway Home and Museum

907 Whitehead Street

Key West, Florida

USA

HemingwayHome.com

Made in the USA
Columbia, SC
22 February 2024

31858512R00067